New York and Nashville houses most of the Ingram employees. We decided to create a book that spotlights some of the popular places the Ingram employees enjoy to going to in both cities. We are spotlighting a few places people like to dine and socialize at when they are in New York and Nashville.

Food Places in New York

Best Pizza

Patzeria Family & Friends 311
W 48th St.
New York, NY 10036

NY Pizza Suprema
413 8th Ave.
New York, NY 10001

A family owned pizzeria that has been around for 45 years. A true originator of the New York style pizza.

Best Restaurant 3 mi Radius from Ingram

KazuNori | 15
W 28th St
New York, NY 10001

KazuNori believe that the experience of eating hand rolls
is truly something special and worthy of its own
restaurant, so we created KazuNori — The Original Hand
Roll Bar.

Los Tacos No.1
229 W 43rd St
New York, NY 10036

LOS TACOS No.1 was created after three close friends
from Tijuana, Mexico, and Brawley, California, decided to
bring the authentic Mexican taco to the east coast.

Best Burgers

Burger Joint
Le Parker Meridien 119
West 56th Street New
York, NY 10019

The Burger Joint concept is based on perfecting the art of grilling – and has been supported by the many awards we are privileged to have won.

Best Vegan Restaurant

Blossom Restaurants 187
9th Ave.
New York, NY 10011

Best Coffee Houses if Wifi Goes Out

Gregory's Coffee 551
Fashion Ave. New York,
NY 10018

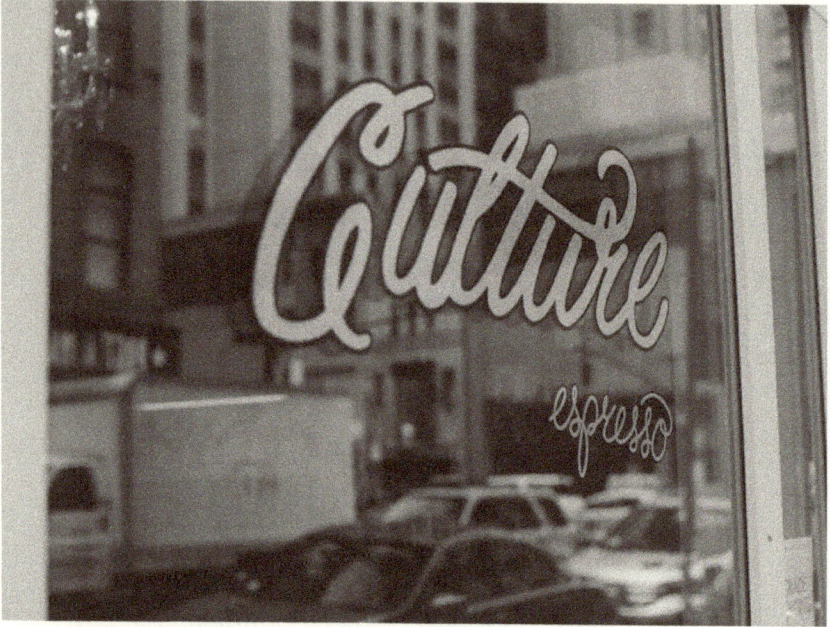

Culture Espresso Bar 72
W 38th St.
New York, NY 10018 Culture Espresso

Best Bagels

Best Bagel & Coffee
225 W 35th St. A
New York, NY 10001

Brooklyn Bagel & Coffee Company 286
8th Ave.
New York, NY 10001

Best Sandwich Spots

Picnic Basket 65
W 37th St.
New York, NY 10018

Entertainment in New York

Best Movie Theaters

AMC Loews 34th Street 14 312
W 34th St,
New York, NY 10001

Regal E-Walk Stadium 13 & RPX 247
W 42nd St.
New York, NY 10036

Best Bookstores

Kinokuniya New York 1073 6th
Ave.
New York, NY 10018

The Drama Book Shop
250 W 40th St. #1
New York, NY 10018

Best Happy Hour

District Social 252
W 37th St.
New York, NY 10018

Juniper
237 W 35th St.
New York, NY 10001

Best Sports team

NY Giants

One of three professional football teams located within the state of New York. The Giants are probably the most known and recognized by people in New York.

NY Rangers

The states professional hockey team. The Rangers made it to playoff as a Wild card team in 2017.

Food Places in Nashville

Best Hot Chicken Nashville:

Prince's
5814 Nolensville Pike #110
Nashville, TN 37211

One of Nashville's famous hot chicken restau- rants.
People travel far and wide to get a taste of Nashville's hot
chicken.

Pepperfire Hot Chicken 1000
Gallatin Ave. C Nashville, TN
37206

Best Restaurant 3 mi Radius from Ingram

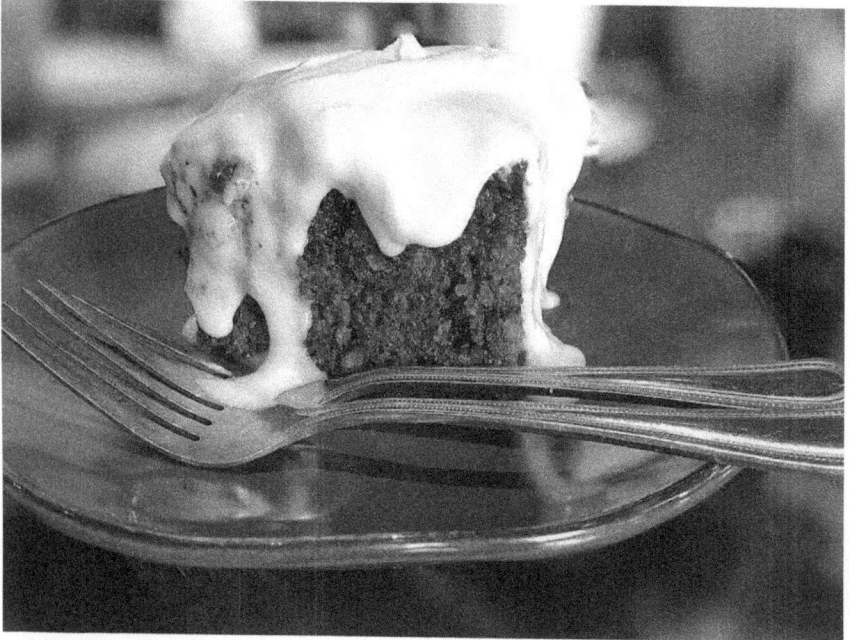

Hickory Falls
999 Industrial Blvd.
Smyrna, TN 37167

Thida Thai
10644 Cedar Grove Rd.
Smyrna, TN 37167

Best Burgers Nashville:

M.L. Rose Craft Beer & Burgers
2535 8th Ave. S #107 Nashville, TN
37204

Gabby's Burgers & Fries 493
Humphreys St.
Nashville, TN 37203

Best Coffee Houses if Wifi Goes Out

Frothy Monkey 2509
12th Ave. S Nashville,
TN 37204

Dose Coffee & Tea
3431 Murphy Rd,
Nashville, TN 37203

Best Bagels:

Star Bagel
4502 Murphy Rd.
Nashville, TN 37029

Best Sandwich Spot

Mitchell Delicatessen
1306 McGavock Pike
Nashville, TN 37216

Entertainment in Nashville

Best Movie Theater:
Belcourt Theatre 2102
Belcourt Ave
Nashville, TN 37212

Regal Cinemas Green Hills 16 3815
Green Hills Village Dr.
Nashville, TN 37215

Best Bookstores:

Parnassus Books
Hillsboro Plaza Shopping Center, 3900
Hillsboro Pike #14
Nashville, TN 37215

Fairytales Bookstore 114
S 11th St.
Nashville, TN 37206

Best Happy Hour:

Saint Anejo
1120 McGavock St.
Nashville, TN 37203

Village Pub & Beer Garden
1308 McGavock Pike
Nashville, TN 37216

Best Vegan Restaurant:

Sunflower Café
2834 Azalea Pl.
Nashville, TN 37204

The Wild Cow

1896 Eastland Ave.
Nashville, TN 37206

Best Sports Teams

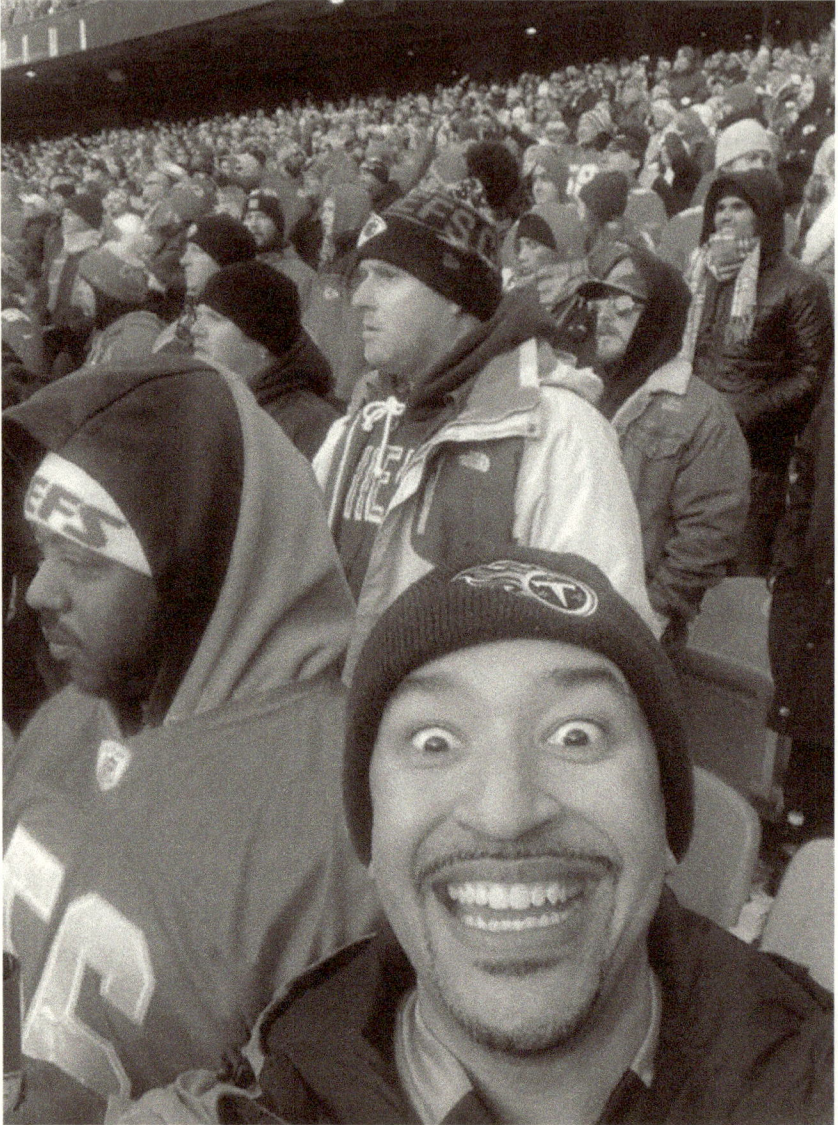

Tennessee Titans
Nashville's professional football team. Titans have finally
made it to the playoffs for the first time in almost 10 years.

Nashville Predators
Nashville's professional hockey team. The Predators made
it to the Stanley Cup final in 2017.

If you are ever in New-York or Nashville come visit some of the places that the people of Ingram love to dine or even hangout at out. Please also explore these cities yourself and add on the places to visit in New York and Nashville.

www.ingramcontent.com/pod-product-compliance
Lightning Source LLC
Chambersburg PA
CBHW031227090426
42740CB00007B/736